TRASH!

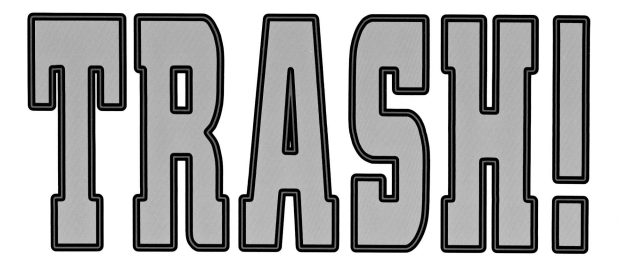

TRASH!

by Charlotte Wilcox
photographs by Jerry Bushey

Carolrhoda Books, Inc./Minneapolis

The author would like to extend special thanks to the following people for their help in making this book possible: Bob Deem, Dan Erhart, Lynda Forbes, Bill Hoefling, Lawrence N. Hicks, Mike Kim, Michael R. Kunz, Ron Larson, Blake & Tara McLean, Terry Miller, John Moreland, Eugene Walters, and Tim Yantos.

The photographs on pages 24 (both) and 25 are reproduced through the courtesy of Donohue & Associates, Inc.

This book is available in two editions:
Library binding by Carolrhoda Books, Inc.
Soft cover by First Avenue Editions
241 First Avenue North
Minneapolis, Minnesota 55401

LIBRARY OF CONGRESS CATALOGING-IN-PUBLICATION DATA

Wilcox, Charlotte.
   Trash!/by Charlotte Wilcox: photographs by Jerry Bushey.
      p.   cm.
   Summary: Examines various methods of garbage disposal, with an emphasis on sanitary landfills but also surveying such alternatives as mass burn and recycling.
   1.Refuse and refuse disposal—Juvenile literature. 2. Sanitary landfills—Juvenile literature. 3. Recycling (Waste, etc.)—Juvenile literature. [1. Refuse and refuse disposal. 2. Sanitary landfills.] I. Bushey, Jerry, ill. II. Title.
TD792.W55   1988   88-461
363.7′28—dc19   CIP
                                                     AC
ISBN 0-87614-311-7 (lib. bdg.)
ISBN 0-87614-511-X (pbk.)

Manufactured in the United States of America

   4 5 6 7 8 9 10 98 97 96 95 94 93 92 91

For those who conserve our resources

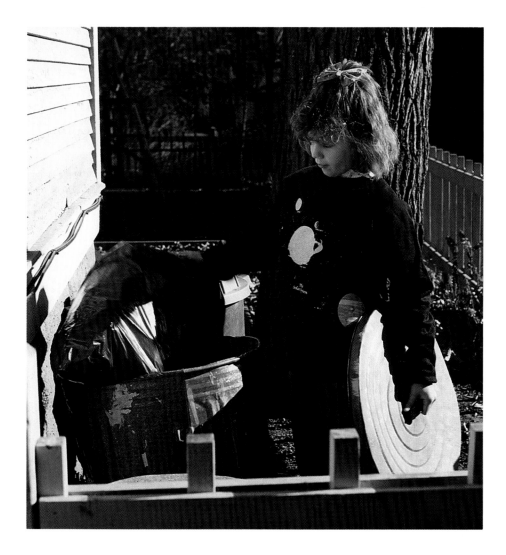

Who takes out the trash at your house? Maybe it's one of your jobs. Even though you may not think so, taking out the trash is an important household task.

Trash, sometimes called **solid waste**, is everything that is thrown away. Some things are thrown away because they are not wanted or are no longer useful. Other things are thrown away because they would be harmful or unpleasant to keep.

If trash is not taken away from where people live, it can cause problems. Animals and insects that are attracted to trash because it contains things they like to eat can become disease-carrying pests. Trash also contains chemicals such as those found in cleaners, paints, and sprays, that can be harmful to people and to the environment.

About 3½ pounds of solid waste are thrown away every day for each person in the United States. That adds up to almost one billion pounds of rubbish per day, or 100,000 garbage truck loads. If that many garbage trucks were lined up on a highway, the line would reach from Chicago to New York! Americans spend over $7 billion every year to get rid of their trash.

Have you ever wondered where the trash goes after it leaves your neighborhood?

The next time you take out the trash, think about the person who picks it up and hauls it away. That person has a very important job.

Rubbish haulers want their trucks as clean as possible to prevent odors and to keep away animals and insects. The trucks are washed often, inside and out. And since a new garbage truck can cost $120,000 or more, mechanics keep them in good repair.

The type of garbage truck seen in most neighborhoods is the rear loader. These trucks work best for picking up household trash such as paper, food, and yard waste. The rubbish is loaded into the truck from the rear, often by dumping out the garbage cans by hand. Sometimes special containers, called **dumpsters**, are used. Hooks on the back of the truck pick up the dumpster and empty it into the truck.

Most garbage trucks have **packers** that compact, or press, the garbage into the truck box. A metal door slides from the rear toward the front of the box. As the door slides, the garbage is pressed toward the front.

Trucks can haul much more trash in each load if the garbage is compacted. A neighborhood garbage truck can haul four to five tons of compacted waste at a time.

The front-end-loading garbage truck is larger than the rear loader. These trucks usually haul trash from business areas or crowded neighborhoods that use large dumpsters.

Front-end loaders work almost the same way that rear loaders do, except the garbage is loaded into the front of the box and pressed toward the rear. Huge forks come down over the truck cab, pick up the dumpster, and lift it over the cab to be emptied.

Large stores and businesses sometimes use **compactors** to pack their trash even before the garbage truck comes. This cuts down on the space needed for storing trash and discourages people or animals from picking through the trash.

Some types of solid waste cannot be hauled off in packer trucks. Builders throw away large pieces of wood, concrete, and other building materials. Factories throw away shipping cartons and large amounts of other waste. This kind of trash is often too stiff or bulky to compact.

These places have **roll-off boxes** for storing and hauling rubbish. Some places are even equipped with special chutes for loading trash.

Roll-off boxes are the size of semitrailers and are large enough to hold a forklift! They are hauled in on trucks, rolled off onto the ground, and left until they are full. Then they are rolled back onto trucks and hauled away.

15

What happens to trash after trucks take it away? Most of it is taken to special areas called **landfills**. There are probably about 15,000 landfills in the United States today.

A landfill starts as a large hole in the ground, usually several acres in size. Trucks drive into the hole and dump their trash.

Then each layer of trash is covered with about six inches of dirt. Every day, more trash and another layer of dirt are added.

After a few years, the hole is filled and becomes level with the ground. After many years, the landfill grows higher and higher and becomes a hill of earth and trash.

The layers of earth and trash must constantly be packed down and leveled so that trucks can drive over the landfill. New trash must be covered with dirt as soon as possible to keep away animals and insects.

Huge bulldozers level the trash and pack it down. Some have giant spikes on their treads that break the trash into smaller pieces so it will pack better.

Giant graders take dirt from other parts of the landfill and spread it over the garbage. Then bulldozers pack the layers down.

These landfill workers have spotted some barrels that could contain **hazardous waste**. Hazardous waste is trash that contains harmful chemicals. If the barrels contain only ordinary trash, they will be buried in the landfill. If it cannot be determined what is in the barrels, they will be sent to a laboratory to be tested. If the tests show that the

The first landfills were called **open dumps**. Trash was simply hauled into a hole and dumped. The garbage was only covered with earth once in a while.

Open dumps can still be found, but most communities have stopped using them because open dumps cause many problems. They are even against the law in many areas.

Animals, insects, and fires are always problems at an open dump, but what's worse is how the water near and underneath the dump is affected.

barrels contain hazardous waste, they cannot be buried in the landfill. Instead, they will be sent to a special hazardous waste disposal area.

OPEN DUMP

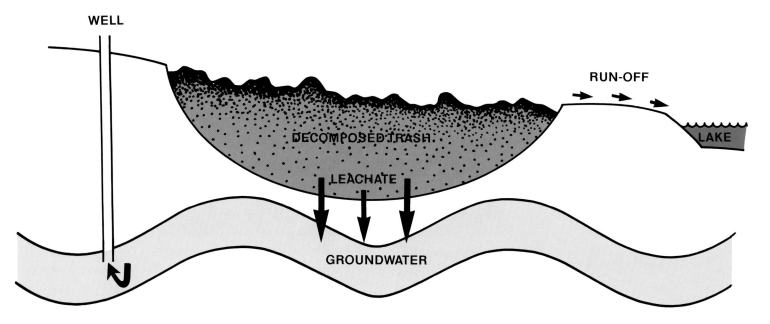

WELL

RUN-OFF

DECOMPOSED TRASH

LEACHATE

LAKE

GROUNDWATER

When it rains, chemicals from the landfill run off into nearby lakes and streams, where they can harm fish and plants.

The garbage sitting in an open dump begins to **decompose**, or rot, and turn to liquid. This liquid is called **leachate**, and it contains many harmful chemicals.

Rain drains down through the decomposing trash and soaks into the soil of the landfill. As the rain soaks deeper into the ground, some of the leachate is carried with it. Finally the leachate reaches pockets of water, called **groundwater**, deep beneath the surface. These pockets of water are sometimes tapped by wells to provide drinking water for homes. When leachate gets into groundwater, it can make the water harmful and unusable.

Modern landfills, called **sanitary landfills**, are designed to keep leachate from leaking into the soil and groundwater. Some landfills are covered on the bottom and sides with a layer of heavy clay soil that is too dense for the leachate to soak through.

Others are lined with large, heavy plastic sheets that trap the leachate and keep it from soaking into the water below. The plastic is made to remain strong and leak-proof for many years after the landfill is closed.

SANITARY LANDFILL

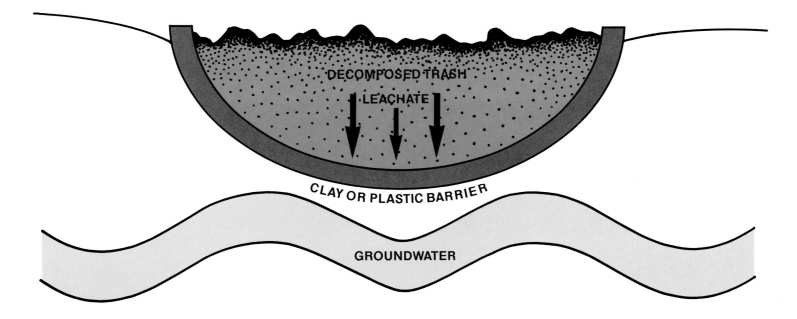

DECOMPOSED TRASH

LEACHATE

CLAY OR PLASTIC BARRIER

GROUNDWATER

This plastic-lined landfill will be full in about 20 years and will hold almost 300,000 cubic yards of solid waste. That would fill almost 1,000 school classrooms!

Drains can be installed in the plastic sheet so that the leachate can be piped out into ponds near the landfill. Bacteria in these ponds react with the leachate to make it safe enough to be dumped back onto the soil.

By the time a landfill contains about three million tons of garbage, something else begins to happen. Some of the decomposed garbage turns into **methane**, or natural gas. The gas forms in pockets at the center and bottom of the landfill. Methane burns very quickly and can be dangerous unless it is removed.

Many landfills sell the methane created by trash for use as fuel. If this cannot be done, pipes are driven into the gas pockets, and the methane is brought to the surface and burned. A landfill containing three million tons of garbage could produce enough gas to meet the needs of about 18,000 homes for 15 years!

Here is a **foundry**, a plant where metals are melted and shaped into products. The metal must be heated to an incredible 3,000° F. A lot of energy is needed to get something that hot. The foundry buys methane gas from a nearby landfill to make electricity to heat the metals. This gas costs less than many other sources of energy.

The methane gas runs huge engines that generate electricity. These engines use 6,500 cubic feet of methane per hour. That much gas would heat enough water to fill over 1,500 bathtubs! (The gas water heater in your home uses only 17 cubic feet of natural gas per hour.)

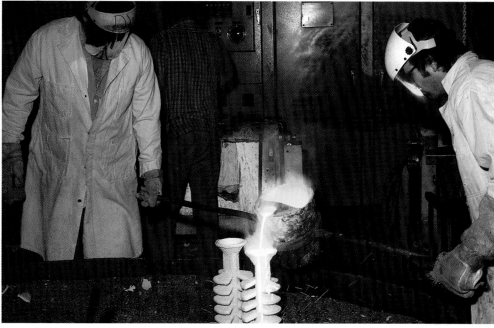

When a landfill gets full or too high, it must be closed. Most landfills today are designed to be used for about 20 years. Then they are covered with about two feet of soil and planted with trees and grass. They can become parks, sports fields, or parking lots. This ballpark used to be a landfill.

This landfill has been in use for 20 years and contains about 3½ million tons of solid waste. Now full, it is about 150 feet high, or as tall as a 15-story building. The area filled with waste covers 65 acres, which is bigger than 100 football fields. The owners might turn it into a ski area in the future.

A few years ago, landfills handled almost all the solid waste in most areas. But land-fills are not always the best way to dispose of garbage, especially in big cities. They cover large areas of land that are needed for other purposes. As landfills become full, new ones must be started, taking up more and more land.

In very large cities, landfills are often located 100 miles or more from where most people live. Since garbage trucks are not made to travel that far, **transfer stations** must be built. There, garbage haulers dump the trash into semitrailers that take it to a landfill. This extra step makes the cost of garbage hauling higher in these areas than in areas without transfer stations.

Many cities are looking for new ways to get rid of solid waste. One method is the **mass burn** process.

Trash is hauled into a mass burn plant and dumped. Items that will not burn, such as refrigerators and washing machines, are sorted out and hauled to a landfill. The burnable trash then goes into a huge furnace that burns at a very high temperature. The heat given off by the furnace can be used to heat buildings.

About two-thirds of the solid waste that is hauled to a plant gets burned in the mass burn process. The other one-third remains as ash and must be taken to a landfill.

Some of the harmful chemicals in the trash are burned up, but some escape into the air. Lead is a substance that goes into the air when food cans are burned. Food processors are beginning to use new kinds of cans that do not contain lead.

Another way of dealing with solid waste is to treat it in a plant that turns it into a dry, fluffy fuel. In this method, garbage is dumped on a floor in the plant, and large appliances and tires are taken out. The trash then goes through a sorting process that removes any metal. Everything that is left is shredded into small pieces. This material is called **refuse-derived fuel**, or **RDF**.

In this process, RDF makes up a little over two-thirds of the solid waste. The other one-third gets recycled as metal or goes to a landfill. RDF can be used as fuel for electric power plants in place of, or along with, coal. Sometimes RDF is compacted into pellets so it is easier to transport.

In some parts of the country, almost one-fifth of the solid waste is yard waste such as lawn clippings and leaves. Composting is a way of treating yard waste so it does not have to go to a landfill.

The grass and leaves are put in a pile. As the leaves begin to decompose, the temperature rises inside the pile—up to 150° F. The heat kills weed seeds and harmful germs. Sometimes nitrogen, in the form of old fertilizer or manure, is added to make the yard waste decay faster. The decayed waste, called **compost**, is used as fertilizer or as potting soil for plants.

In some parts of the world, composting is done in large processing plants that treat paper waste along with grass and leaves. The compost produced is used by farmers as fertilizer on fields.

One of the hardest waste materials to get rid of is old tires. They do not decompose well in soil and are hard to compact or shred. If they catch on fire, the flames are very hard to put out. When burning, tires give off dangerous fumes. Research is being done to find ways of recycling tires instead of throwing them away.

Almost everyone agrees that **recycling** is the best way of dealing with trash. Recycling means finding a use for something that would otherwise be thrown away. This idea is becoming more important as landfills become full and the cost of getting rid of trash increases.

The recycling process begins at home, where different types of waste can be sorted. The three types of trash that can be recycled are paper, glass, and metals. If they are sorted out before being thrown away, they can be taken to recycling centers.

In many areas, garbage trucks like this are equipped with separate bins for different types of waste.

At the recycling center, the items are prepared for shipment to factories that turn them back into useful products.

Only about one-tenth of all solid waste in the United States gets recycled, mostly because people do not take time to separate items before throwing them away.

Research is being done to find new ways to use trash—as insulation, building materials, fertilizer, and feed and bedding for farm animals.

Reducing the amount of unusable trash is everyone's job. This can be done by buying things with less packaging and in containers that can be recycled. Grass clippings and leaves can be composted or left on the lawn. Writing paper can be used on both sides.

Perhaps you can think of other ways to cut down on what is thrown away. Maybe someday you will even take part in research to find new ways to use solid waste. Getting rid of our trash is an important job.

GLOSSARY

compactor: a machine that presses material tightly together, usually so that the material will take up less space

compost: a mixture of dead leaves, grass, and other organic materials, partially decomposed, used for fertilizer and potting soil

decompose: to rot or decay

dumpster: a steel container for storing trash, usually designed to be picked up and emptied by a garbage truck

foundry: a plant where metals are melted and shaped into products

groundwater: water that is found beneath the surface of the earth

hazardous waste: trash that contains chemicals that may be harmful to people or to the environment

landfill: a special place where solid waste is buried

leachate: liquid formed by the decomposition of waste in landfills

mass burn: a process of burning solid waste at a high temperature

methane: gas that is formed by the decomposition of wood, grass, and other organic materials; natural gas

open dump: a place where solid waste is dumped and left uncovered for a period of time

packer: a machine on the box of a garbage truck that compacts the trash

recycle: to reprocess material such as metals, paper, and glass

refuse-derived fuel (RDF): solid waste that has been shredded and processed into a dry, fluffy fuel

roll-off boxes: mobile boxes the size of semitrailers that are used to contain oversized trash

sanitary landfill: a landfill designed to keep leachate from leaking into the soil and groundwater

solid waste: trash from households and businesses, mostly made up of paper, food, containers, and yard waste

transfer station: a place where garbage trucks from big cities take trash to be dumped into semitrailers that take the trash to landfills